For my mother and father.
Thank you for always believing in me.

ISBN 978-1-66780-990-8

Printed by BookBaby, in the USA.

First edition 2021

BookBaby.com

Anthology of an Adventurer
by
Rachel Powers

Part 1

I have never felt so deeply and completely encased by a single city as the way I feel in the city of Chicago. I have lived in the suburbs all my life with the city looming over me in all its supposed gloriousness. I've never seen this glory. I've never seen anything but walls. Walls that surround me and pull me tumbling down into the center of a pit to prepare my demise.

Stepping out of Union Station onto Jackson Blvd. invokes a sort of claustrophobia that I know I need to escape. I cannot remain here where I am suffocating at the bottom of this pit. The "glorious" buildings loom over me and extract every last drop of freedom running through my veins. Each building I pass has me looking up to the sky waiting for blue to take over and save me from the walls, but they only grow taller. I must fight to escape. I need to get to where I belong and away from this city so consumed by ever-growing stone walls.

I can't think of anything I have in Chicago that's worth staying for. I have a family and I have City Boy, but family is family no matter where I end up in the world. City Boy is everything I want, but he's not what I need. It was an adventure to get to know him, but if I stay here with him, this city will tear down everything I am every time another wall is put up. The only reason I am still here is because I've been waiting for that one moment of revelation to tell me "Yes, this is where you need to be." But I have already had that moment.

I found that one moment on a rock in Central Park and I have never been the same since then. My life was changed, for the better or worse I don't know, but that is where I belong. Falling asleep on that rock, I felt like I had a home at last. I woke up surrounded by strangers, some who were also taking naps in the beautiful scenery and some who were just having lunch. There were a couple of men in suits sitting on rocks and eating lunch together. There was a family, the little girl chasing a butterfly and the little boy running in circles with his race car toy exclaiming "ZOOM ZOOM!" I was a tourist

in the park, surrounded by strangers, watching
them have a normal day, and I was home.

I can't help but laugh at myself now for
thinking at the time that waking up on a rock in
Central Park was home. It made coming back to the
Chicago suburbs feel like I was a shelter dog
being put back in its cage after a moment with a
prospective family. I was put back in my cage and
I feel the repercussions of it every day. I can't
go on like this. I can't keep myself locked away
when I have felt what it is like to be freed.
Every day I remain, I am more and more encased by
the fear of disappointment. I am not afraid of
disappointing anyone but myself. I cannot live my
life knowing I have grown up with the
expectations to move away and yet remain trapped
in this city.

When I was a kid, my favorite Disney movie was Pocahontas. I loved that she was so independent and strong, but mostly what I loved about this movie was the way she viewed nature. "Just Around the River Bend" has always stood out to me and was the song that I couldn't help singing in my high-pitched little girl's voice. She starts off with the line "You can't step in the same river twice, the water's always changing, always flowing." Growing older in a culture of stone surrounded by construction, I sought the rivers. I sought the flowing water to watch nature at its finest. Watch the peaceful simplicity of life in the water. The older I got and had more time to watch a river flow and just examine the way it moves, I realized that a river is never truly the same in one moment as it was just seconds before.

The water is flowing and taking sediment from the bed with it. Fish are constantly swimming back and forth. The water temperature changes over the course of the day determined by the sun and the temperature of the air brushing over the water. When it rains, the water gets colder and runs faster. The water is never the same. It will never return to exactly how it was before. It can never truly be the same river I walked in before.

The same goes for the stars. The Earth rotates around the sun at about one degree per day, changing the stars that we see and making different seasons possible. Within a single night, however, the change is more visible to those, like me, who will lie on the cold asphalt of a pitch-black parking lot and stare up at the sky, watching it change. Every twenty minutes, the night sky rotates approximately five degrees, shifting the position of the stars. Because of this, different stars are available at different times of the night.

Perseus could just be peeking up from behind the pine trees, pointing to Andromeda hiding beneath Cassiopeia. In just an hour in summer, he could be a quarter of the way across the tilted sky. Scorpio is only visible for a little while in the Northern Hemisphere. He resides just above the southern horizon line and glows the prettiest of all the stars as he is a giant orange light that sometimes chooses to flicker. I never miss the opportunity to see him for the couple hours he appears as he is and always has been my favorite of all. He will glow steady and bright one night and flicker the next. Sometimes he is yellow and sometimes orange. He is beautiful but he is transient.

Just as the stars and the rivers can't remain the same, neither can I. I can't be stuck in the same place and do the same things every day for the rest of my life. I would go crazy with lust for a new view and a new me.

I remember the time we walked around the campground. City Boy and I held hands and walked blindly. I wouldn't let him use the flashlight so he kept his eyes on the ground, squinting into the dark. He didn't understand the easiest way to navigate is to look to the sky. There's a world of wonder up there, blinking and twinkling at us constantly, but he didn't see it that way.

He didn't see the way the stars invite our eyes to watch them glow and they show us the way. He saw their beauty but he didn't see the way they could direct us back to camp if we let them. He wanted to use the flashlight and drown out the beauty of the stars until he could sit back down in the chairs by the fire and lean back comfortably to look up. It doesn't work that way. You have to look up.

My father used to say, "If you're always watching where you walk, you might miss something incredible." He would say this right after he tripped on a log on one of our hikes, but despite

the phrase being tied to his clumsy hiking, I
found it true in various aspects of my life.

I've begun to feel trapped and engulfed
here in Chicago, like I will never escape the
bottom of a pit. I am surrounded by walls that
loom over me day after day and I am entombed at
the bottom. But maybe it's not the pit that is my
problem. Maybe I'm looking down too much and I
don't give myself enough time to admire the
stars. There aren't many stars here, but I've
never appreciated the ones that are. Maybe it
isn't the quantity of them present, but the mere
strength they possess to shine through all the
pollution consuming Chicago.

Back in Michigan that night, a meteor fell
that gathered both of our attention. We watched
it explode and light the sky like nothing I've
ever seen before. It was beautiful. It was
bright, it was magical, and it was a pure dream.
It was freed from its orbit and taken on a new
expedition. It entered our atmosphere and there
were two explosions. The first explosion, the one
that caught our attention, was when it broke
through the atmosphere. It was bright like a bolt
of lightning, and the meteor faded to leave only

a trail of light behind it. The second explosion took place only a fraction of a second later when it had gained enough speed and it exploded once again. I could see the fire erupt from within it and break free, engulfing the entire rock and feeding on the air surrounding it. The first explosion made him look up. The second explosion held us rooted where we stood in awe. We remained frozen on the path watching the fire consume everything until nothing was left. Just a fraction of a second later and there was nothing more to see. It was gone. The fire had burnt out.

The sky had captured him at that moment and he finally walked with his head up to the night sky.

"She followed me on Instagram." I could hear the solidarity in my own voice as I tried to keep steady.

His breath was heavy on the other side of the phone. I had interrupted his time at the gym, and he always hated that; but no matter when I said this, it wouldn't end well. "What do you mean?"

"I followed her back and I creeped on her photos a little." I wanted so badly for him to understand, for him to know what I saw. "Can you tell me where you were last weekend?" *I'll give him another chance to be honest*, I told myself. *He'll tell me.*

"I was working. You know that." He had the same voice he got every time I questioned him at an inconvenient time. I could physically feel the weight of his eyes rolling and his palm slamming down on whatever surface had the misfortune of being next to him.

"Was she at the concert you were working at?" He sighed heavily, loudly, irritated.

"Yes, she was there." My eyes fell to look at my fingers as they played with the bottom of my shirt. *His shirt.* My room was dark with no lights on and the sun was just about to set, so I could only see the silhouette of my hand blending into the oversized dark tee shirt. "She was attending the concert, but I didn't talk to her. I promise."

"You promise?" My voice was small. Unrevealing. I didn't know how to make it anything else when all I wanted to do was scream, but the pressure of avoiding a breakdown kept my vocal chords on hold.

"Yes, I promise. I saw her from the sound booth and she came up to say hi, but I did nothing but wave." He sighed more relaxed this time, and I knew he thought I bought it.

"So you didn't have your arm around her waist and take a picture? That's not you on her Instagram?" I had caught him. He kept his silence. "You said you'd tell me. You said you'd be honest if you talked to her." My voice grew more confident as I spoke. "I told you all I cared about was being honest with each other and you couldn't."

"Oh shut up!" He snarled into the phone and I could envision his face turning a deep purple just like my father's every time I made him mad. "Why can't you just mind your own fucking business?"

"This is my business. When it involves you lying to me it is my business."

"No. It's not. It was never your business."

"So every time you told me who you weren't comfortable with me talking to one of my guy friends without your permission it wasn't because you were jealous?"

"No, I-"

"So every time I stopped talking to a close friend, it wasn't because you wanted me to?"

"You don't understand-"

"So when you told me I should do that for you, it wasn't because I would get the same respect from you? Cause, wow, was I wrong then." My voice came out harsh and stern. My body was shaking, but luckily my voice did not resemble the pain that resonated through every bone in my body.

I had never cared so deeply for another human being; the thought of opening myself up to the realm in which the word "love" truly existed had always disturbed me. I had never understood the appeal in having someone to rely on, someone to be there for, and someone to cry on when I needed them. It was a foreign land that he had opened the door to and I foolishly entered.

"You're too much of a bitch. You're too sneaky. You're too boring. You're too clingy. You rely on me too much." He spat words into the phone one after another as if they were all meant to form only one sentence. He kept talking, kept sneering. He kept deepening his voice. "You're nothing to me. You never were. I kept you around as a placeholder. I like her. I want her."

He stopped speaking for only a moment. A moment in which I processed every word he had just said and I realized just how much I was glad we were on the phone. I knew that, if we were in person, I would be crying. I would be afraid. I wondered if I would be the locker that I could hear him slamming his hand into over and over

again in the background as he spoke. Instead, I
remained calm in appearance and cold in my
voice.

"I spoke to her. I messaged her and we
talked about the two of you." My voice came out
small once again. "I needed to know her side
before I asked you."

"What did you say?"

"I asked her who she thought I was and she
said your ex. She said you told her we broke up
over a month ago. I told her that, if we did, it
sure wasn't communicated to me."

"Why the hell would you do that? Now I have
to try to explain to her how crazy you are."

"I guess she would be the one to worry
about if I never really mattered." I wanted him
to say something. I wanted him to apologize and
tell me he was just mad. That he didn't mean any
of it. That I did matter. That he wanted to talk
about this. That he wanted to work things out
with me. I had spent the last year and a half
with him and opened my life up to him and I
wasn't ready to let a girl who lives a hundred
miles away ruin us.

"I have to call her. We can talk later."
Silence ensued. The phone fell from my hand and I
made no effort to pick it up.

He was the reason I never wanted to love.
He was the reason I had closed myself off from
the outside world for so long. He was the reason
I never trusted another person. He was the reason
I felt that, to open myself up to love, would be
suicide of a worse form than that which I so
desired. He was the reason I had thought the word
"love" to be nothing more than a word that had
lost its meaning in an age in which that was all
a human being craved. He was the reason for all
of this which seemed pointless now that it was
over.

He was nothing. I was nothing. In a world
of nothing is where we existed and I was a fool
to think it more. The worst part was that, after
our conversation, after the hatred with which he
spoke to me, I felt okay letting him go.

You know what I love most about the forest?
The way I can fall in love without so much as a
word being spoken. The way I feel is all that
matters. I have always been deeply in love with
the woods in a way that most wouldn't understand.
It speaks to me. I can hear it whispering secrets
to me with every splash the fish make as they
jump up from the water. The leaves tell me which
way to go when I'm lost after abandoning the
trail. The wind hums calming songs when I need a
friend and don't know where else to go.

I guess that's all I've really wanted out
of the people I surround myself with.
Specifically, what I really want out of my
relationships is to find a forest within a
person. I don't know if that's possible. I don't
know if I will ever find someone who can make me
feel like the forest does.

Somehow, City Boy did at one point.
Somehow, he was able to lead me down the right
path when I lost my way. He told me little

secrets I had no interest in, but found it amusing to hear anyway. He was able to calm me when I found myself needing a friend. He continues to be all of this now too, but the difference between him and the forest, the one thing urging me to move on, is that he is too consistent.

He tells me secrets of others but he doesn't tell me the ones that matter, his. He tells me everything I need to hear and then some, but he tells others too. The difference between the forest and him is that he is here. He is in Chicago. He is always here and he treats everyone the same. I don't know if that's supposed to be a good thing or not but it's not what I want.

I want the forests because I can go anywhere and still find one not too far to comfort me in times of need. The forest is there for me and has constantly changing parts for me to explore. The trees grow bigger and fall, their trunks giving out under a bolt of lightning. The water gathers and carves new paths after a storm. Animals dig new holes and claim new territory. One tree blooms before the others. One tree won't bloom at all this summer. It's always changing in one way or another. City Boy is always the same.

He's caring. He's comforting. He's here. But he's always the same. It's the same comfort, the same caring, forever the same place for me to find him. He doesn't understand how achingly boring that is.

He never changes, even between who he's with at the moment. He will care the same for me as he does for someone he may not even care about at all, and he doesn't understand why I don't believe him when he says he loves me anymore. He can't be the forest that only has to be there to comfort me. He can't be my forest no matter how leafy green his eyes are unless he can learn to treat me differently from the beautiful blonde from class in need of a ride or the brunette friend wanting a drinking buddy in her apartment. He can't be my forest because he can't change.

I don't even know if I would want him to change. It would be like humanity claiming a forest as its own and cutting down everything that makes it beautiful. He is the same and treats everyone equally and that makes him beautiful and caring and comforting and boringly, *achingly* consistent. I need a forest where the comfort is always new in its own way and the caring is ever lasting as long as I respect it.

The forest has always been my home and maybe I thought City Boy could be my forest because he asked me to share it with him. He asked me to and he loved me, so I did. I showed him everything beautiful about it, every little thing that makes me fall in love over and over again with nature. I showed him everything, except that it's always changing. I needed him to see it for himself.

Adventurer: noun; a person who has, enjoys, or seeks adventures

I guess the difference between him and I, a
City Boy and an Adventurer, is pretty simple:
he's okay staying here. He was born and raised in
the Chicago suburbs, same as me, but he has no
desire to leave. I've never wanted to stay.

Ever since I can remember, I have thirsted
for travel. I have been staring out plane
windows, watching the shadow of the wheels touch
the ground and felt the windows shaking as the
brakes do all they can to slow the plane, since
before I can remember. I've always loved being up
in the air. Something about being at an elevation
human beings are not supposed to know, made it
inviting and even more appealing to me. He closed
his eyes because he thought we would crash into
the Hudson when we landed in New York City. He
had only been on a plane once before, to Miami.
He hadn't travelled much at all.

I can't imagine being stuck in one place my
whole life, but that's all he has ever wanted.
He's always wanted to live in Chicago and spend

his life working here. He never had an interest
in even seeing New York, or Michigan, or anywhere
else, until I begged him to go. He told me New
York had nothing for him and he didn't care to
see something that would ultimately mean nothing
to him, but I made him go with me.

I've been to New York more than a couple
times now, and it's the only city I have ever
loved. I think the reason I love it so much is
because it's so big, so it would take a long time
to see everything. There's always more to see and
I can be engulfed and swallowed happily by
Central Park and its beauty rather than the walls
I have become so familiar with in Chicago. With
Chicago, I can't seem to find anything new to
explore. I haven't seen it all, but it's all the
same. Business buildings and scattered artworks
line most streets in the city and the suburbs are
littered with nothing but home after home with
strip malls and parks that the city calls
nature.

The beauty of traveling is that I can never
see the whole world. Even if I have gone to every
country and seen every coast of every ocean from
every city in every country that lines those

oceans, I will never have seen everything. It's impossible to see everything in the world before I die and that's exactly the beauty in it. How can I sit still in the same city for my whole life when there's an entire planet out there? Chicago is just a small corner and he can show me everything great about the city, but I will never understand his desire to stay, but he says this is home. He can't leave because this is where he belongs because it's the city he knows and the city he's comfortable in.

It's odd. It's almost like traveling has always been the only option for me. As a kid, I ran around the woods near my house and climbed the trees in my backyard just to feel like I wasn't near a city. I've never wanted to be the typical teenage girl in my high school that went downtown in a large group just to take a picture in front of the "Bean." I never saw the "Bean" until City Boy made me go because we go to school only blocks away. I never thirsted for the city everyone I knew rambled on about. To me, hearing about it was enough.

City Boy has always cherished the moments he spent with his parents downtown. His family

went to North Avenue Beach for a family outing.
My family drove until we lost cell reception and
set up camp. We only grew up ten miles apart down
the same highway and yet we've grown up with
completely different views of the world. I'm
still shocked that we have been able to share
these views with each other. City Boy told me
that I have instilled a bit of a travel bug in
him. I've been too shy to tell him I'm starting
to see what he loves about Chicago and what it
holds for his future. It took a while for me to
understand, but he is business and Chicago is
full of business, so he does belong. I am nature
and adventure and always searching for something
new. I do not belong and never will.

There were many times that I should have
seen how we don't belong. It started with the
cities. It started with my love for New York and
his passion for Chicago.

He loved the underground music and the
1920s speak-easies. He loved the crowd that could
afford to live such extravagance that they played
the pre-Great Depression crowd perfectly. He
drooled over them and their lavish dress. A Monte
Blanc pen was all he dreamed of one week; and at
the end of the week, he bought it. He could
afford their lifestyle just as well as any rich
bachelor in 1920s Chicago.

I loved the sky. I loved looking up and
counting the birds and spotting eagles' nests. I
loved breathing in the cold air over Lake
Superior and letting the icy waves crash over my
bare toes. I loved watching barges pass through
the canal down the street from my childhood home.
I loved New York. I loved the way I could go back
as much as I desired and I was never bored. I

spent my time relaxing and exploring the small things in my city. I found my niche in the city that never sleeps and I still revel in it every time I save enough money to board a plane.

He was Chicago and too lavish.

I was too in love with simplicity.

We don't belong.

We never did.

Every winter, instead of seeking somewhere warm to thaw off during spring break, my family always searches for good deals on ski trips. It had been a while since I was able to join the family ski trip, but this year I decided to ditch school and work for a couple days and bought last minute plane tickets to join my mom on a flight to Salt Lake City. She was to meet my father, brother, and my brother's fiancé in Park City. It probably would've been just another trip of skiing through the endlessly tall evergreen trees and riding the chairlift with three complete strangers for miles back up the mountain, which I did do, but only for one day on this trip, because my dad tore his ACL on the first day he was there.

My dad and I have the same sense of adventure that burns within us. If we are in a setting we haven't been before, then you can find us wandering somewhere in the woods or climbing a cliff to get a better look. He is the one who taught me to climb trees when I was little. He taught me about the stars and instilled enough patience in me to watch them long enough to see them rotate through the night. Our love for nature and longing to see everything it has to offer has never allowed room for something as small as an injury to hold us back. I knew he wouldn't stop the vacation because of his knee, so my parents and I planned a road trip through the Wasatch Mountain Range.

The rental car GPS backfired on us, however, when it took us down a road that wasn't exactly a road so much as a snow-paved path for snowcats and snowmobiles. My dad tried to back off onto a real road but, instead, got the car's back end buried in four feet of powder snow.

We met a couple strangers who helped us try to shovel the car out after laughing at us for being stupid tourists. It took a lot more than just them shoveling and my dad and I pushing the car. My mom was in the driver's seat trying to see if the two front wheels would grip anything on the path at all. In fact, it took so much more effort that even the snowcat one of them drove couldn't tow it out. The other had to call his friend to bring his Pistenbully. The Pistenbully struggled a little bit, but eventually succeeded in releasing our rental car from its almost-grave.

After freeing the car, the one with the snowcat, Mike, invited us to his cabin just up the mountain. He drove us three miles up the mountain on the snowcat. On the drive to his cabin in the middle of nowhere, with zero cell reception, Mike's almost empty Bloody Mary threatening to spill, and a 9mm glock on his hip at all times, we learned that he works in the psych ward in Salt Lake City Hospital. He had a couple psych ward friends up at his cabin for the weekend and he couldn't wait for his wife and friend "tall Tony" to meet us when we got there.

My mom kept making jokes about episodes of crime shows that start out with strangers trusting someone who turns out to be a psychopath. Perhaps Mike was actually a patient at the hospital psych ward, but the visit was actually a lot of fun. It was one of those cherished few moments where my parents got to just live in the moment, which my way-too—careful brother never lets them do. He flipped out when we got back to the condo and lectured us on "stranger danger" before his girlfriend told him to shut up.

The drive back to our car was my personal favorite part. Mike and I had talked about guns a little bit in his cabin and, on the ride back, he saw a no trespassing sign about fifty feet away and stopped the snowcat. He handed me his gun and told me to shoot it because he "thought he saw a couple trespassers." I stuck my arm out the rolled-down plastic window and pulled the trigger. Even with my arm out the window, the sound was deafening. My ears were ringing for a couple minutes afterwards as Mike congratulated me for hitting the sign dead-center. "Pretty good for a rookie," he laughed. It was my first time holding a real handgun and it felt incredibly good. My hand was shaking from the weight of the gun and my entire body shook from the adrenaline pumping through my every vein. The gun had started out cold, but as I handed it back to him, it was my hand that was cold. From that moment forward, for the rest of the night, I don't think the smile left my face for a single second.

My brother stuttered un-interpretable words after this story and went to my parents asking how they could let any of this happen. He is a twenty-three year old med student and I don't think he has ever had a pure, reckless adventure. I don't think he knows how to. Sometimes I wonder if he knows that the best adventures are when you barely know where you are. You learn the most about an area by having to figure out the situation.

Despite my dad and I being so similar, he has always wanted me to be more like my brother. He thought my brother was the perfect child, but I'm not like him at all. I need adventure and my brother needs consistency. He hates change and he loves routine. I can't go more than a couple days with a routine before I start losing interest and abandon the whole concept. I crave something new and something freeing. My parents got to live that experience with me for once because my brother wasn't there to offer the "safe" route for the situation. Instead of my brother's influence directing my parents' thoughts, the three of us got to have an adventure of our own.

That's what I have always craved and what my
brother always yells at me for searching to find.

I don't know what to do or how to feel anymore. I want to be happy but everything I do here tears me down and I don't know how to be better.

I don't even know where to start.

Do I start with City Boy? He makes me happy for a day and then I find myself in tears. He loves me when he's here but he's a different person when I'm not in sight. He changes too much. And yet not enough. He's too afraid of changing the person that I've never seen to really be with me. He's afraid to lose the part of him that just wants to be young and free.

We have different ideas of young and free. My idea of young and free is to travel and live how I please with the people who mean the most to me. His idea is to be surrounded by a lot of people and be connected to as many people as possible before he settles with what he truly wants. I don't need to be surrounded by many people to know what's good for me.

Do I start by traveling? I want to see the world. I want to experience as many cultures as I can and learn the way the Earth moves in every place. I want to feel the differences between the wind in the Appalachian mountains versus the French Alps. I want to watch the waves rush up to shore from a bungalow in the Maldives and experience how they feel as I lay in the sand on the shores of Ireland. I want to know every part of the world before it's too late.

I'm done sitting in the corner because I'm afraid to step out of my shell.

And yet, for as long as I stay in this town, in this city, in this state, I will never change that. I can't be the girl who will talk to anyone. I can't be the girl who is confident enough to go up to someone and make my presence known. I can't be the girl who will tell someone they can't mess with me. I won't let it bother me, but I'll never say something. By default, it ends up bothering me even more.

In Utah, I was confident. I went off on my own when I didn't feel included and I had fun. I was who I know I can be and I loved every moment of it. In Utah, I was me.

I am me every time I go to New York. I am me when I walk down every street in the claustrophobic, construction-littered, beautiful city. In Central Park, I can stand on my own two feet and feel like I am whole without reassurance from someone who matters. I didn't need City Boy to follow me even though he was there. I didn't need him to hold my hand every time we went through a crowd. For once, I was the one stopping to make sure he was there. I didn't actually care if he was there or not. I just didn't want to be rude.

If I can be myself in places so different from each other as New York and Utah, then why am I so defeated by the walls of Chicago?

I knew the city hid its different faces
well. I knew that, in order to find those faces
and discover the truth about what lies in the
darkest of corners, I'd have to learn how to pry
my way into the places I would never belong.

Just as the city hides, City Boy hides just
as well.

I had come to know many of his faces. He
bears the sign of a Gemini, but I never put too
much faith into Astrology until that night. He
had shown me so many different personalities,
there was a new one for every group of people he
met, but this one was the deal-breaker. I found
myself for the first time pulling away
voluntarily rather than subconsciously.

The face he bore was not anything like the
guy I thought I knew. He was a different being
entirely.

We had a good time. His friend bought us
tickets to a concert down south as a double date
in exchange for rides there and back. The night

was perfect. Three music nerds and a music reviewer made for a never-ending stream of conversation about the artists and City Boy's company until it took a spin we all saw coming because she was too much a part of their lives.

I knew he lied to me about her being a part of the company and about her hanging out with them when I wasn't around. I was used to his lies; it didn't phase me. What did phase me was the silence that followed and the dark cloud that descended upon my car while we were still two hours away from the city.

We continued in silence for a while until I decided I needed caffeine. We stopped at a gas station and I asked City Boy to come in with me and pick out snacks for the rest of the ride while I got us energy drinks.

"I know you're all friends," I said. We were crouched in an aisle, sifting through flavors of chips. "I don't care if her name is mentioned."

He didn't look at me. "I don't want to fight. We don't need snacks. We're almost there." He stood up and walked over to the fridge to grab four drinks.

"I'm not trying to fight. I'm trying to not end a good night with a shitty car ride."

He didn't answer. His silence irritated me more than opening the car door to hear half of a word cut off by silence and the immediate use of cell phones. The three of them texted each other the rest of the way into the city. Our silence was only broken by City Boy offering to drive since he knew where their apartments were and I didn't.

Something in his tone, whether it be the cold, apathetic chill it sent down my spine, or the way it boomed over the vacuum we had become accustomed to the past hour and a half, triggered the worst of my sarcasm. We dropped off his friend's date before dropping her off and I spent the time in between telling her things I had picked up on how to know if a guy is cheating, or if he has too many secrets. I told her that City Boy and I were a perfect example of why it's better to stay broken up after the first heartbreak because it only gets worse.

I could tell she wasn't happy and neither was he, but I didn't care. The long silent ride had given me a reason to believe the girl whose name was mentioned wasn't just a thing of the past. She still wasn't just a friend.

"I don't understand why you have to act like that." His jaw was tight and I could hear the anger in his voice as he pulled away from her apartment.

"I don't understand why you can't just tell me what's going on? Though, I should know by now, that honesty from you would be a miracle." I knew this response would irritate him. He liked to believe he was the perfect liar. I let him believe that I didn't know anything about a lot of his secrets, but I'm not an idiot. He knew it, too, which is why he got so mad whenever I tried to talk about things.

"I don't want to fight." His jaw was getting tighter. His voice came as a pure snarl now. "But you just had to embarrass me in front of my friends."

"Me? Embarrass you? So having a girl I already know you still lie to me about come up in conversation and the entire car dies like a forbidden topic just came up isn't embarrassing? The three of you made it quite clear there's something I don't know about." He kept speeding up. My small sedan in need of new tires was reaching almost 100mph and his foot kept pressing harder. "Slow down! You're going to get pulled over."

"Don't fucking talk to me!" The car pressed on faster down the highway. I looked over at his face and in the passing light I could see an expression I had never seen before. He was mad. He was more than mad. His eyes were unblinking and his hands gripped the wheel so tight his knuckles were reflecting the streetlights. His nostrils were flared and his jaw was glued shut.

I took a deep breath and came to terms with having to let go of my attitude if I wanted to calm him down.

I've been truly scared only once in my life prior to this night and I can remember the exact feeling. The way my heart wanted to escape out my throat. The way my lungs wanted to collapse before they had to witness anything more. The way my blood heated up every vein in my body. The way my instinct knew what to do before I did.

His obsession with music did not fail him in this moment, but aided in his anger. My playlist seems to always know where my life is headed and at this moment it did not help the situation. *The Approaching Curve* by none other than my favorite band, Rise Against, had come on and City Boy reached for the dial. He turned the volume up as high as it would go and we listened to the words Tim uttered.

I clenched my eyes shut as our exit grew increasingly closer, dangerously too fast. He slowed only slightly in the midst of the sharp curve and I opened my eyes to catch the speedometer drop as low as 80mph and I felt the wheels beneath the passenger side threaten to release the pavement below. I shut my eyes once more.

"Stop the car." I spoke as softly as I could when all my lungs wanted to do was scream. "Stop the car." I repeated the phrase a couple more times until I felt the jolt of him releasing the gas pedal. I opened my eyes and looked at him to find tears streaming down his face. We gradually slowed until he pulled off the road and stopped the car.

In a high school parking lot, I whispered, "We're done," and opened the door of my own car and ran. I ran up the steps to the front door and collapsed against the brick wall. I stayed there breathing heavily until I heard the slam of a car door. I looked over to where he had parked to watch him walking away.

I stayed there for a while longer as the effects of the adrenaline wore off and I found myself too tired to drive. I slept in my car that night and when I got home I told my mom I fell asleep at City Boy's house. I didn't know what to tell her. I didn't want to tell her what happened; I couldn't. I didn't know what I felt about it, myself. All I knew was that he had yet another side to him that I didn't like, and this time I wasn't sad or mad or upset at all about it.

The night before had numbed my feelings for him. I had known him for years and never seen him like that. He had always had a calm demeanor, no matter what, but he was different. I knew he had changed over the last year, but the extent to which he had changed had not appeared to me until that night.

And I wanted nothing to do with it. I wish I could say it truly was the last time I let him make me feel that way.

I've been driving past Midway Airport every day on my way to school in Chicago and it's become increasingly more difficult to keep driving. There is always traffic between the last exit for the airport and the two before it, giving me plenty of time to imagine where I would buy a ticket to if I got off the freeway.

I'd like to say I would go somewhere exotic, somewhere I would never have thought to go, but I've imagined almost every corner of the world. Sri Lanka has always intrigued me with its history and its beauty. The Maldives are in that region as well with floating bungalows on the ocean. Central Africa has animals and rain forests I have never seen before. Russia has the beautiful St. Petersburg I have been aching to see. Scotland has StoneHenge and the Forest of Dean.

Perhaps I should choose somewhere I know I would have a friend or family to stay with. Sina has been begging me to come out to Switzerland

and she would show me Germany and France as well. Giulia is moving to Paris in August and wants me to help her move. She's living just outside of Florence right now. I know I have family in Waterford, Ireland that I've been wishing to meet.

I have so many places I can go. Wherever I want to go, it would be easy enough to leave. I think about pulling off and entering the airport. I imagine myself walking through the automatic sliding doors, with only my school messenger bag, and asking for the next ticket to wherever my heart desires. Whatever country I desired the moment I opened my mouth is where I would go.

I wonder how long I could stay there before realizing it was time to come home and be responsible. Would I ever come home? Would I stay there, in a foreign place and learn the language, study the area, and call it my own? I imagine that I would make a name for myself wherever I landed and never have to come back to this city of walls that has held me hostage for so long.

Dear Mom,

The funeral today was beautiful. It was
odd, but it was amazing in its own depressing
way. I've never been good with funerals, but you
know that. I avoided the seemingly endless stream
of them in high school, escaping by only going to
the wakes and the occasional mass. I had to
support my classmates so I had to be at some part
of them. God, high school took a lot of friends
away. I suck at these things, but I guess
everyone does in some way, right?

Well, my method of survival today was to
look everywhere but at my dear friend. It was
hard to see him like that… I couldn't stand
seeing the always up-beat, fun-loving, life-of-
the-party with bloodshot eyes and lacking perfect
hair gel. He still had some gel but it wasn't the
perfectly brushed back pillow above the buzzed
sides it usually is. His eyes looked like they
were each stung by bees. Yes, multiple. He was a

perfect image of a grieving man. And I couldn't even look at him without wanting to cry.

I don't know what I would do if I were him. I like to think I'm strong, but I'm positive that he was a million times stronger than I could ever be. He never shed a single tear through the whole funeral. He gave a fantastic speech, talking about all the best memories he had with his mom and the things he will keep with him forever. It was touching. I couldn't think about it. I couldn't listen to it because it made me think of you and if I were in his position, so I thought about my own funeral.

Her casket was beautiful, but I want oak. That was my first thought about the whole event. I want oak, and I don't want the cement surrounding me. I want to be free of walls when I go. That way, all I have is the oak casket separating me from the earth.

You know I've always been about nature. I've always loved being surrounded by trees or sitting on a river. You and Dad used to take me to the Quarries a lot when I was little. I loved how we always carved our own paths through the woods whether we were on bikes or hiking. Even in

the Upper Peninsula, Dad and I would set the
canoe down and explore some part of the forest
the canoe wouldn't fit through. He always left
that out of the story when we got back to camp
and you asked how it was because he was worried
you'd be mad about us going off in places we
weren't supposed to be. We always have a good
time up there; no work, no internet, no friends,
and no cell reception to distract us from the
surrounding environment. I want to be like that.
I want nothing to distract me from nature when I
am buried. No cement and no metal casket. I want
oak.

I want to be buried in a tree like I spent
most of my childhood up in a tree. You both hated
that I spent so much time in our willow tree
that, when we moved, you planted only oaks. I was
jealous of those oaks. They got to be so high up
and feel the breeze at a height I would never
reach. They got to know what it felt like to have
birds sing to their beauty and the beauty of the
day. I couldn't climb those very easily. I
managed when you and dad weren't around because
you would've been mad, but I always wished I
could've gone higher. Maybe if I'm buried in oak,

then I can finally feel what it's like to be one.
Maybe I will dream about all the memories it has
from its time as a tree. I know you will think I
am ridiculous, but I'm a dreamer. Just like you,
Mom.

You painted all those forests and rivers
and I have them all hung in my room because we
dream the same. I remember watching the
Tahquamenon Falls one summer when we stopped on
the trail because you wanted to see it. We shed
our shoes and our socks and walked out into the
river and looked upstream. We watched the water
rush past our ankles and continue down, hurdling
over every rock and stone in its path. We felt
the algae growing over the rocks and forcing the
water to run smoother, faster. That moment with
you was when I decided I wanted to be an artist
or a writer, right there in the river surrounded
by forest.

Some of the most precious moments in my
life were in the woods. As I grew older, I would
go to the Quarries and just lie down next to the
water when we were fighting or I had a bad day
and didn't want to talk about it. The trees

always seemed to comfort me, so it only seems

right to be buried in one.

Love always,

Adventurer

The desire, the thirst, for the world has always run deep within my veins and pushed me to crave a broader view of the world around me. I've always known that to truly get away I needed to do it alone. I needed to find the strength within myself to reach for my own goals rather than settling for the goals of those important to me.

I realized that this past summer.

I had been living for everyone I loved with the attitude of a spoiled brat. I've made myself up to be the goals of my mother and pushed myself to inadvertently follow in my father's footsteps.

However, I don't want to make the same mistakes. I don't want to confine myself to a life in the city I have been aching to escape. I don't want to fall in love and be trapped where I am. Trapped in the life I loathe.

I made up my mind as a young girl to live on my own, for myself and my parents, never allowing anyone to hold my heart for too long. If

I wanted to truly escape, I had to change that goal to live for only myself and only hope everyone else is on my side.

I moved out.

I got promoted at work.

I got straight As.

I booked a vacation in Ireland alone.

I listened to everyone tell me my first trip overseas should not be alone; I should go with a group. I went alone anyway.

I booked more vacations. Some with friends, some alone.

I met someone. A cop. A profession that I, myself, once aspired to become until my creative side took control completely and changed my course.

I didn't have to allow him to have my heart because somehow he already had it. He had a part of me from before I even knew his name. I had never seen him before, but he recognized me. We had crossed paths when City Boy was my world and my head hung low in defeat every time I stepped into the mysterious so-called glory of the city. It almost seemed like fate. But who believes in that? I never have.

I'm a loner. A dreamer. A traveler. I am a girl who has spent my life closed off to the people around me except the select few who have always stood by my side no matter what. They hold my heart. No one else. Especially not a cop, someone who has already built his life in this city bearing so many walls.

Now, I'm sitting on a plane alone to Dublin. I just watched the Northern Lights out the pitch black window. They shimmered and faded and danced back to life over and over in colors of green and purple. It was beautiful.

I had dreamed of seeing the lights ever since I was a child and my father told me about them. He explained that they were created by light passing through the atmosphere at different speeds. That's where the color came from because each color traveled at a different speed. Purple is the fastest color. Red is the slowest. The scientific name for the lights is the Aurora Borealis. A beautiful name for a beautiful sight.

Just a couple days ago the cop and I had discussed taking a trip to Alaska together to see the Northern Lights. I wish he was here so we could be nerds together rather than me pressing my face against the window alone, creating fog in the shape of oversized nostrils.

Maybe independence doesn't have to be so lonely. This cop won't last, but I don't have the heart to tell him I'm just an adventurer passing through. I'm not meant to stay in a city of walls. This city isn't mine, but adventures don't always have to be in the silence of my own crazy life.

In the few years I have spent as a young woman, I have done nothing more than try to escape Chicago. It has always felt more of a cage than a home to me and I knew even as a child that I would never be able to live this way happily.

I have gone on adventure after adventure searching for the perfect place to call my home and found nothing but the forest, the sky, and Central Park to satisfy me. The realization had pushed me to believe that I am nothing but a wandering soul. I would spend my days either claustrophobic in the city Of Chicago or wandering endlessly through yet another part of the world. The idea is almost too romantic. The prospect of being able to live my dream traveling and never have to call anywhere my home is just that: a dream.

I have come to realize the truth of the emptiness I feel so deeply. It is not a city or country that I have been searching for to call home. It is not the endless travels that will sustain my happiness. Those are merely placeholders.

The truth is that I have come to know a different sense of the word "home." One that I would not have foreseen would come into my future, but the world is a strange place and not everything is as predictable as I have become accustomed to.

The cop has only been in my life a short while and yet, somehow he has become more of a home than I have ever known within the people I surround myself with. More than City Boy's family, and more than the campus ministry leader with whom I was so close in high school.

He has not come close to being the comfort with which the forest has always provided me, but when I am wrapped in his arms, I know I'll find my forest someday. The forest, to me, means more than just an adventure. It is and always will be a place that offers peace and serenity.

So, maybe, the home I have been searching for does not have to be in the sky or in the forest. It does not have to be in Manhattan or Dublin. I can be anywhere to be home.

It has now been almost a year and a half since my last entry. My need for adventure overruled what little remaining passion I had for finding a place to last in the city of Chicago. I could no longer bear the thought of putting my life on hold and suspending the hunger for another exploration.

The cop understood. He understood that my life was not meant to remain in sync with his. He understood when I told him I just wasn't willing to stay.

I have come to terms with the city of Chicago. Once I had enough distance from City Boy and took it upon myself to take the L around to different villages, I became my own tour guide and was able to settle in that *this* is my city. I may not love it, but it is mine.

I no longer have the burning desire to purchase a one-way ticket. I will leave the city, but I will take my time and find the place I am meant to call my home. I guess, I've grown up.

I've matured from the angst-riddled teenager that followed City Boy all over Chicago waiting for the day I didn't feel suffocated. I thought the city was my problem but I know now, it was the boy. It took a Cop to show me the truth in the situation and to show me that I could love a city almost as much as I love the forest.

Even as I write this, I am sitting alone on Montrose Beach in Chicago. I have taken up sailing as a hobby and learned to love the city for its beauty from across the Lake. Once my friend and captain arrive, I will head once more into the waves to take my place beneath the sails. I will be surrounded by both the city and nature in my own perfect serenity until the time comes for me to take my final adventure and leave my city and its walls in my past.

Part 2

I moved to Arkansas. I drove 700 miles with everything I owned crammed into my midsize SUV. It was packed. I was packed, my apartment was empty, and I wasn't turning back. I drove with a fury in my bones that I hadn't felt for a very long time. The fire that burned within me consumed my entire being so much so that I don't recall very much of my journey. I don't recall the food I ate, the roads I drove, the turns I took. Did I eat at all? Did I stop and drink my coffee at a coffee house or did I simply drive through a fast-food joint and grab food and coffee all in one?

I know I must've turned as thoroughly as I know I drove the roads. There must've been many highways and overpasses. I know the hills I must've passed and the cliffs looming with red stones over the highways in Southern Missouri. But I can't recall that specific drive. I arrived in Arkansas to find a home I didn't know I'd love

and yet the feeling of freedom overtook my
ability to recant the moments that passed.

All I remember is the moment I realized
just how big of a step I had taken. I moved home.
Most would feel more trapped than they had
before, but I felt free. I was finally released
from the walls, constantly growing ever taller
and ever stronger, threatening to break down
every piece of myself I was able to put back in
place over the course of my adult life. I was
free from the paranoia, looking over my shoulder
every step I took. The feeling I was never going
to run far enough away to escape the mistakes of
my past. I was no longer drowning in a sea of
concrete. I became engulfed, instead, in a
freedom more full than the comfort of Central
Park. I stepped out onto my parents' driveway in
Northwest Arkansas and I felt further from the
cage of Chicago than I had in Dublin. I had
nothing to fear and nowhere left to seek.

I don't need the memories of the places I
ate or the coffee I drank. I don't need to recall
every turn I took. I'll never drive it again.
I'll never find myself aching for the moments I
should have been second-guessing my decisions. I

tasted freedom a long time ago, and I have been plagued with ever-growing reasons to leave. I've been surrounded for too long with the walls that just never stopped sprouting from the ground and barrelling me deeper into a depression I didn't know I owned. I found strength in a moment of crazy fearlessness and I escaped from a world I never would belong.

As free as I felt, the anxiety that should have pierced me somewhere along Route 66 found me as I unpacked my clothes and filled my closet. I had been living a life of freedom for only a few hours when I realized the full extent to which I had changed the course of my life. I cried as I hung my shirts. I found myself angry and I couldn't pin why. My mother came and hugged me. She gave me a piece of advice I had heard many times over the course of my teenage years as I switched schools and debated the direction in which to carve my path. She told me that growing as a person isn't easy. But escaping is. Escaping to a life I didn't know was the healthiest way to find who I am and for the first time, I had my chance. She told me I'd learn who I am and who I need to be in order to make my way and end up where I am meant to be.

My mother, the woman I had longed so badly to have a glass of wine with and watch stupid TV shows, had once again proven to be the piece of my life that I had been missing since they moved away. With this piece, I could finally begin to rebuild myself without the walls waiting to tear me back down again.

I grew tired of lusting for a new view and took my chances. I found a life in Northwest Arkansas. The trees, the hills, and the lakes- it drew me into a world I had never thought to explore. My parents had moved the year prior and I found that I enjoyed driving through the Ozark mountains to visit them. While packing for a week-long trip, I decided to pack a little extra and take everything. I would miss a few things and people, yes, but what was I truly leaving behind? Walls and skies that never seemed to stretch as far as my eye wanted to take them.

The Ozarks, though, had cliffs and stones to walk out on and imagine just what lies beneath me. I could close my eyes and smell the air and be exactly what I never thought I'd feel fully and truthfully. Freedom smelled of campfires and stung like an icy breeze over cool waters. The sun pierced through the open sky and straight through the cover of leaves offering shade to

warm my skin where the wind threatened to offer
the idea of a jacket.

This freedom came with an outcome I had not
quite anticipated. I missed home. I missed the
city and the memories it held. I missed the way
the train station made me hesitate and look
around as though never sure of my surroundings. I .
missed the way the city sidewalks were uneven and
never quite the color they should be. I missed
the walls and I missed looking up to watch them
fade away, taller than my eyes could follow. I
missed the little neighborhoods where I had grown
accustomed to disappearing in a sea of people.

I had my own little sea now. I had new
walls that grew on their own with rain and soil
and covered the sun with roofs of green. I had
new sidewalks littered with roots where I always
watched to avoid stepping on a turtle or a snake.
I had new worries to pay attention to when
checking my surroundings. Animals crossing the
trails and spiders spinning webs across the trees
offered a new version of paranoia to my life. I
had a new version of disappearing. Far away from
cell reception and anxious for the next outlook,
I discovered a freedom I'd never known.

I was completely alone and utterly happy. I knew absolutely no one and was lost everywhere I turned. I had exiled everything I knew at home in Chicago and walked into a new life, completely unprepared to take on the next chapter of my existence.

I found work at a county jail, the first
law enforcement position to offer me a chance and
the best choice I had to make. Things started
falling into place from the moment I left
Chicago, and now, I had a chance to prove myself
in a career I had always dreamed about. My life
became everything I had hoped it would become. I
found work in a career I was passionate about and
was shown opportunity after opportunity to prove
myself worthy.

I found friends at work and friends in my
parents' neighborhood. I was surrounded by nature
and surrounded by those with the same interests
as me. I found comfort as I drove through the
mountains and into town to go to work. I found
comfort in learning more about the people I saw
everyday at work. I found myself making an effort
for the first time in a long while to be the
absolute best I can be. My life meant more than a
passing glance now. I meant more to the people I

was surrounded by than I had ever imagined could be possible.

At the jail, I found myself crossing danger every day, and yet, I was never alone. I was hesitant at first, recalling the many times I walked through the city and found myself having to learn how to defend myself with nothing but the knife in my back pocket. I recalled being put in more positions of danger alone than I ever cared to mention to anyone I knew. I was alone then. I was alone and vulnerable. At the jail, I had people I could trust. I had friends who would have my back no matter the situation. I found confidence in myself and trusted that I was finally where I am meant to be.

And I met him.

I found work at a county jail, the first
law enforcement position to offer me a chance and
the best choice I had to make. Things started
falling into place from the moment I left
Chicago, and now, I had a chance to prove myself
in a career I had always dreamed about. My life
became everything I had hoped it would become. I
found work in a career I was passionate about and
was shown opportunity after opportunity to prove
myself worthy.

I found friends at work and friends in my
parents' neighborhood. I was surrounded by nature
and surrounded by those with the same interests
as me. I found comfort as I drove through the
mountains and into town to go to work. I found
comfort in learning more about the people I saw
everyday at work. I found myself making an effort
for the first time in a long while to be the
absolute best I can be. My life meant more than a
passing glance now. I meant more to the people I

was surrounded by than I had ever imagined could
be possible.

At the jail, I found myself crossing danger
every day, and yet, I was never alone. I was
hesitant at first, recalling the many times I
walked through the city and found myself having
to learn how to defend myself with nothing but
the knife in my back pocket. I recalled being put
in more positions of danger alone than I ever
cared to mention to anyone I knew. I was alone
then. I was alone and vulnerable. At the jail, I
had people I could trust. I had friends who would
have my back no matter the situation. I found
confidence in myself and trusted that I was
finally where I am meant to be.

And I met him.

In second grade, my science teacher had us study how chicks hatch. We watched the eggs for weeks wondering when they'd crack. I enjoyed watching them throughout class. I've always been terrible at keeping my attention span focused on what I'm supposed to be doing. The eggs and the endless possibilities that raced through my brain kept me from learning until they hatched. I remember staring uninterruptedly at the tank. I can recall the warmth from the lamps sitting overtop the screen. I wondered if they were warm enough, or if they were too warm. What would happen if one burnt out? Was it all for show? Would we come back from the weekend and find no light and no baby chicks?

When the eggs finally hatched, I vowed never to eat chicken again. I held a chick in my hand. Just thinking about it I can feel the fur, so new and soft, wrapping the baby in its own blanket. Until recently, I kept my vow never to eat chicken. Still, I cannot think about the animal I am eating while I consume the meat.

I've become accustomed to ignoring the animals I pass on my way to work. I watch the road with concentration like I've never known as I pass by farm after farm. Cows graze the fields and lie down to take in the warmth from the sun. They drink from ponds and step in the water to cool themselves on the hottest of summer days.

I found myself curious as to what a cow looks like up close. Growing up so close to a big city, I've never seen animals that couldn't be kept inside or on a small patch of land. I walked up to a fence at the County Fair grounds and waited until a cow approached. They're so much bigger and more beautiful than I could've imagined. Their fur is so thin and their ears so big. I found myself in awe of a creature I enjoyed devouring so thoroughly.

I no longer avoid watching the cows as I drive by. I cannot eat beef after watching an animal so beautiful, but I am learning. I am learning the mentality required to live a life so near the creatures that taste so good. It's a

life I am not accustomed to, but a life that
requires adjustment is a life I want to live.

I have traveled the country and then some and never felt pure happiness. I have found myself aching to be somewhere other than wherever I am time and time again with no hope for appeasement. The dull ache that I have felt so dearly for the duration of my teenage and adult years has been absent lately. I haven't searched for a plane ticket nor a cabin in the mountains in quite some time. I haven't taken my car and driven until I lost my way in another state since I found my way to the Ozark mountains.

Instead, I've taken to the trails. I've run trail after trail and looked out over the lakes from cliffs I'd love to dive off. I've swum off the dock at my parents' home and floated to let the sun revive my energy. I've taken to the boat and found waterfalls and caves to explore. Then dove back into the water to avoid the snake whose home I had unintentionally invaded. I've found new adventures within the area I live and no longer seek to escape. I've become comfortable in the small adventures that take me deep into the forest only miles from my home. I have found adventure and a home in the same place.

I take to the woods when I feel overwhelmed and alone to find my friends in the nature that surrounds me on a daily basis. I have come to know the dangers that arise in the creatures I pass by. I've come to know the identifying features that label each snake as poisonous or aggressive. I've come to truly enjoy the pauses in my busy day while I watch a snake slither up the hill and retreat to its space under some leaves or a branch. I've learned to live a life worth living.

Explorer: noun; a person who investigates unknown regions.

I cherish those nights he and I planned to workout together. I cherish the nights we never lifted weights. I love my workouts. I love to build strength and push myself harder than I had the night before. But these nights, we met at the gym. He was always there when I walked in, so I quickly put my gym bag down and gathered a barbell and plates. I set everything up and began lifting. These nights I cherish, however, we began talking instead. We hadn't quite known each other for very long at this time, but I, at least, knew I wanted more.

We spent hours sitting on the gym floor talking about our lives. He grew up similarly to me. He spent most of his life alone, trying to find where he belonged and ended up here, working in the jail. He spent hours on his own at a time, hiking, running, and aching for new views. He grew up in Arkansas riddled with trails and paths to explore, but always lusted for a new view.

I told him about my adventures. He told me I was crazy for exploring Dublin on a moment's notice entirely alone. I told him he was crazy if he hadn't taken chances in life. I was an adventurer. My adventures are how I survive. He explained to me that, while he had never taken the risks of jumping on a plane and taking off to the next destination available, he walked off trails and found new paths. When given the opportunity, he took "the road less travelled by." He was an explorer.

The Explorer helped me to build a family tree dating far back to where my ancestors originated. We discovered pieces of my family that I didn't know existed. We discovered that I come from Norwegian descent. I became interested in the facts that surrounded my family history.

We were Vikings. We lived in rural Norway and sailed ships across the seas. My ancestors lived a violent and grand existence. I finally found the link to my love for water. I found the answers to questions I had about myself that I was reluctant to ask. I am an adventurer by blood and the sea rages within me. I will travel all my life and never feel satisfied. I will consume everything this world has to offer and I will drink it in volumes beyond compare.

He wants to come with me. He aches to explore the earth every opportunity we get, and he will be by my side through it all. For the first time in my life, I believed him. I'm

anxious to share my adventures with him as he has
already shared so many new trails with me.

We've explored caves and lakes I didn't
know existed. He took me down trails that weren't
marked and we found areas that weren't meant to
be hiked. We were adventure and exploration. We
found happiness and comfort in the silence of the
forest and made friends with the creatures we
passed. I had found the answers to why I ache for
an adventure every step I take, and he was a
forest in which I could walk a million miles and
still be satisfied.

The Explorer had a secret. He waited to
introduce me to a piece of his life until he knew
I was just like him. He ached to find new
territory and constantly sought out new
explorations. When he found that I share the same
lust for adventure, he took me flying. I had
never quite laid eyes on a plane so small that
still functioned. I had never expected to be
stepping on the wing of a plane that spanned only
as long as I am tall. I took one step up and
walked on the wing in order to sit beside him
with all the controls in front of us.

We sealed the doors and windows and that
was it. We took off and flew low over a farm. I
watched as we gained altitude and everything
below became like a painting. He asked if I was
nervous before we took off. He asked if I was
sure I wanted to go, if I trusted him to fly
something so small on a windy day. I couldn't
find the words to describe how excited I was. I
simply said yes. I've always loved planes and

being high in the air, where humans weren't meant
to travel. I longed for the freedom of the open
air. I longed to find peace above the clouds.

As we flew, I became less excited and more
anxious to just go further. I wanted to fly as
far as we could go, but we didn't have a
destination. He asked where I wanted to go, so I
asked him to show me everything he thought I
should see. We flew for a while as he pointed out
important Arkansas landmarks. Eventually, we flew
along the lake and circled over my parents'
house. It looked so small and unrecognizable. It
seemed as if nothing was real from so high up. I
wish we didn't have to land.

The feeling of absolute freedom the air
offers is like a freedom I've never known. Even
sailing cannot compare to the weightlessness of a
plane. Running the trails cannot give my legs the
freedom that my eyes took in. Escaping from the
ground with nothing but the one who means the
most to me was an adventure I will forever
relive.

Working at the jail became monotonous. I
went to work with the same routine each day and
grew tired of watching people pass me by in the
worst moments of their lives. I despised viewing
people in moments of weakness, trying to act as
though they had everything figured out. It became
exhausting to put on a front to appear as though
I truly didn't care. I tried to be that person,
but it wasn't me.

I found that I wanted to help the people
who weren't really bad at heart; they were
misguided. They were lost in a world that ran on
money and bitter hearts. They fought to survive
as best they could, and ended up deeper in a hole
they couldn't climb out of in the first place. I
lost track of how many people I watched cry
because they felt like the world had abandoned
them. I offered words of comfort and solace, but
I could only offer so much. Not everyone I
crossed was a lost cause. Not everyone I spoke to
and listened to their stories would spend their

lives thieving to survive. All they needed was someone to listen and help. But I couldn't help.

I found myself wishing that I had more to offer and more to do for them. I searched for ways to show people that they could make more of themselves and never have to come back. Some, I never saw again. I can only hope that they took my advice and went in search of a lawful method to solve the issues they faced. I can only dream that I had made a difference when given the chance. My coworkers called me soft for doing so.

The Explorer is the only one I can talk to about work who shares my views. He understands what I mean when I say I don't want to ruin who I am for a job I thought I wanted. He sees me for who I am and has guided me and talked me through how to help without jeopardizing my job. But I want out. I want to work where I don't feel as though I am breaking down everything I love about myself to be someone that I thought I could be. I long for a career that I can truly make a difference and be happy while I do. I can't continue to be someone I'm not in order to someday become someone I wanted to be. It would be the suicide of my soul.

I began searching for jobs, not quite caring to stay within law enforcement. I searched job site after job site. The Explorer did the same. He said I had taught him to see the depression the jail had instilled in him, and I lifted it from his shoulders. He no longer sought to hold the anger in his heart that working years at the jail had brought to his life. We were both going to leave.

For the first time since my days in the spotlight on a stage, dancing my heart out with my closest friends, I can say that I am truly happy. I began in a pit of construction and walls being built around me like I was stuck. I was trapped in quicksand and instead of falling deeper, my cage was put up around me. I stood in place and watched as brick by brick was added to bury me in a despair that I couldn't escape. It began with words. It began with a boy that I thought was my world. It began in a childish dream.

That's what I was. A child. A child who thought I knew what I wanted and who to be in order to get to where I was going. I thought I was a writer, a traveler, a tough girl who could get through anything. A girl who could escape my fears by simply fighting for what I wanted. I was wrong.

The only way to escape a world in which walls were all I saw was not to fight to stay

where I was. I wasn't meant to be happy
surrounded by a cage. I was built to fight, but I
was fighting for the wrong cause. I fought to be
someone and stay somewhere that I needed to
escape.

I'll never quite understand why it took me
so long to come to the decision I made that day I
packed up and moved. But it took me to a life I
hadn't anticipated. My life has changed entirely
in just a year, but I have grown to understand
exactly what true happiness feels like. I've
found myself in the world in which I belong and
have found answers to goals that I had and paths
that I thought were mine to travel.

I guess that goes to show how even the most
hungry don't always know what they need. I used
to be hungry for adventure. I used to spend every
waking hour just waiting to escape, but I never
took the leap. I never made the effort unless it
was only halfway planned out. I thought
spontaneity was a dream and that it could only
take me so far. I didn't know it'd be my saving
grace.

The baby steps that I took, the trip to
Dublin, the unfamiliar roads I drove, the woods I

lost my way in, they helped me to see all that I missed in the moments I spent in Chicago. I was never meant to stay. I felt at home on Lake Michigan amongst the waves because my ancestors wanted me to travel. I felt the urge to go further because I was never meant to turn back. I did so out of safety. For as long as I yearned for adventure, I only ever chose the safe route. I came back to Chicago each time I left and tasted the sweet air of freedom. I turned around and drove myself back into the cage that I desired so thoroughly to escape.

I took a chance. I took a step far bigger than anything I had ever done before. Moving away from the home that I had grown up in and all my family and friends was a step I was scared to place my foot on, but it became easier to take the next few steps once I did. And those next few steps are what led me to be the strongest version, most me, of myself that has ever been.

The Explorer wanted to go hiking on one of the hottest days of the summer. He persisted, and I craved nature, so we went. It was a trail we had hiked only once before together, but he knew each path like I knew the trails back on the outskirts of Chicago.

The trail was short, but the view was amazing. A small creek ran along parts of the path and branched out to follow in some directions. There was a short wooden bridge that brought us over a piece of the creek. He took my hand and dragged me in one direction off the main trail. We followed along a cliffside with the creek bordering the other side of the thin trail. It had become quite a habit by now, so I spent the majority of our hike talking a million miles a minute.

I was engrossed somewhere in a conversation about grasshoppers, mostly dragged on by my own frantic style of thinking, when I stopped. Hanging from a tree was a picture frame, it contained two photos of the Explorer and I, and below it was a sign that said, "I love you." It was not nearly the first time I had heard or seen the words from him, but I carried on. I was drawn further down the trail by the sight of other frames hanging along the trail.

It had been eight months that he and I had been together. We had gone on adventure after adventure. I had learned about his family and his past. I loved it all. I had made memories and friends in Arkansas, but still, he was the center of my attention.

We turned around at the end of the path and walked back in the other direction. There was a waterfall down one path, but he guided me down one I hadn't traveled before. We approached the water. A trail brought us down below another wooden bridge and we walked beyond. Continuing along the stones that lined the water, we came to an opening.

Just in front of me lay stones creating a circle of pavement just before the water opened into a basin and the waterfall was just beyond. Upon the stones lay a cloth. Perfectly laid out were pictures of us. He and I in every way our

favorite moments were captured in time. Rose
petals were scattered across our path, where
roses could never have grown. Upon the stones,
just above the cloth, were two words I had not
anticipated.

I turned around to find my Explorer, on his
way down to one knee. A box, a perfect little
wooden box in his hand. I don't remember the
words he said. I don't recall putting a ring on
my hand. I only recall the overwhelming feeling
that nothing could be more perfect. Our perfect
place, a perfect path, a perfect dream. The water
in the background and a family of small children
shouting their congratulations across the basin.
It was all a fantasy.

We left the trail and went to see the
people who mean the most to us. His grandparents,
parents, and my parents. One big family. One
family for the rest of our lives. It was the
first time they had all met and the most
wonderful experience I could have possibly
imagined. I had everything I needed, everything I
had searched for, everything that meant
everything to me was right there in front of me
and I had no idea what I was truly missing until

I had it all right there. A perfect life amidst perfect people. A wonderful little town in the corner of a state I barely remembered ever learning anything about in school. A gorgeous range of mountains with lakes everywhere I look. It was all mine. And the most wonderful Explorer stood in front of me, ready to take on the world together.

I took a leap of faith in retreating from everything I knew in order to remake myself in a new state. I followed my parents to a place I had barely a crumb of an idea about belonging to, and found myself starting a life that would be long lived in happiness. I was hesitant to step into a relationship while I was so new to the environment and still attempting to act as though I wasn't terrified to end up in another cage. I couldn't possibly have the audacity to escape a life of walls to sink into a town where I could watch as the same walls were built taller around me. My first big leap of faith gave me a lucky break in finding a home amongst the trees.

My second leap of faith brought me to an ending even sweeter than the one to which I was still adjusting. My expectations in a man had always been so strict in order to truly fall for someone. I needed a forest. I needed to find a man who belonged to the forest and felt the spirit of nature all around him. I needed an

Explorer to aid in my search for new adventures.
I had not expected an Explorer to be laid out in
my way and placed by fate in the middle of every
road I tried to cross. I had not anticipated
being swallowed whole by an emotion I had never
felt before.

In times past, I had closed myself off to
any idea of something real. I had shut down
entirely while I got to know exactly who it was
in front of me. With my Explorer, I wanted him to
see me for everything I am. Broken but kind.
Scared and out of place, but I was in search of
happiness. He never saw those things in me. He
saw someone crazy and tough with a heart of gold
and a brain to make anything come true. He saw
more in me than I did myself and he showed me
just how to make myself shine.

My Explorer was more than a leap of faith
in my timeline. It was more than a leap of faith
that brought me to Arkansas. I was broken down to
nothing in Chicago and given only what I deserved
out of my life there, so I would leave. I was
forced to leave and by the time I did, I had
nothing. I had less than nothing to remain in a
life run down, so I left. I had nothing to lose

but pride. I had only myself to blame for allowing myself to stay so long and revel in my mistakes, but if I hadn't, then where would I have ended up? If I had left earlier, I wouldn't have fled to Arkansas. I don't know where I would have been, but Arkansas and the Explorer would never have crossed my mind.

A life in Arkansas was just what I needed. A career in a jail was where I was meant to begin my journey, whether or not it worked out for me in Law Enforcement. Because it brought me to him. It brought me a life where I didn't feel I needed a reset button to rewind every decision I've ever made. I'm happy. I'm entirely satisfied in a town where I can hike forever and never be bored. I can run and find new outlooks. I can swim to new caves I hadn't explored before. I can live amidst trees and water and spend my days off work lying on a dock and watching the herons perch on stones across the way. My Explorer will be with me through it all.

Our newest adventure was just about to begin.